Say WHAT?

100+ Questions to
Ignite Conversation &
Spark Dialogue

JODEE BOCK

Say WHAT?

100+ Questions to
Ignite Conversation &
Spark Dialogue

Jodee Bock

Bock's Office Publishing
1945 49th St S
Fargo, ND 58103

Use these questions liberally, but responsibly.
Don't ask them if you're not really interested in
the answers you may get. Because then you'll just
make people mad.

ISBN: 978-0-97857224-2
Printed in the U.S.A.
2nd Edition

For all those who are curious enough to ask the tough questions, and courageous enough to search for their own answers.

Categories

Intro	9
About Learning	17
About Strategy	21
About Change	25
About Addressing Difficult Situations	29
About Redirecting Others' Behavior	33
About ME!	37
Non-Questions	41
Appendix	47
Prayer From Napoleon Hill	58

Intro

When I was a little kid, I was very curious. And inquisitive. And probably really irritating. In fact, I remember in fourth grade asking what I thought was a very important question because my always-searching brain needed the answer:

"Teacher, why is a dollar sign an S with a line through it and a cents sign a C with a line through it?"

I was genuinely curious.

Looking back, that question must have been the straw that broke my poor teacher's back. I remember her saying, in frustration, *"Jodee, look it up!"*

Even though it's not what she said, what I heard was:

"If you have to ask so many questions, it must mean you don't know how to find the answers for yourself."

"You're bothering the class with your silly questions."

And, probably most damaging to my 10-year-old self: *"Only dumb people ask questions."*

So while I stopped asking them out loud, that didn't mean my brain shut those questions off.

Over the years I've learned a lot about questions, and realize I'm not the only one who wonders things and wants more information. While questions have gotten a bad rap from those who believe as I used to that they reveal stupidity, it's the context around which the questions are asked that can make them provocative, evocative, irritating, frustrating, or ground-breaking.

One of my favorite authors is Peter Block, who in addition to being a top-notch consultant, is also an author and a community builder. Among the books I love most is *The Answer to How is Yes: Acting on What Matters* (2001). It was in this book I first discovered that, as Peter tells us:

> *"Transformation comes more from pursuing profound questions than seeking practical answers."*

Profound questions can provoke action, reduce confusion, and open people up to discovering ideas and possibilities they didn't even know they had already inside themselves. When you ask a profound question – of others or of yourself – you can take a conversation and understanding to a whole new level.

Igniting conversation is less about who is right and more about the connection. And dialogue is very distinct from discussion, which comes from the same root as percussion and concussion. When you invite someone into dialogue, each of you agrees to suspend previous assumptions in order to learn from each other. Even if both parties don't realize that distinction, you can be the instigator on an energetic level just by asking a question instead of making a declaration or a command.

CAUTION:

In any form of communication, intent and commitment are key to positive results. Albert Mehrabian's research shows that in any conversation or communication dealing with feelings or attitudes, the total message gets conveyed most accurately when the visual, vocal, and verbal channels are in alignment.

Mehrabian's way of stating this was:

Total Liking = 7% Verbal Liking + 38% Vocal Liking + 55% Facial/Visual Liking.

-Albert Mehrabian

Asking one of these questions without getting clear on your own intention and commitment – being aware of your own desired outcome – may not be as effective in transforming the relationship, as Peter Block stated earlier. The best opportunity for that transformation is to be aware of each party's intentions as much as you can be: your own, for sure.

So in your hands you hold a tiny treasure which will help you in your own pursuit of profound questions. You already know where the questions will be most helpful ... you just may not have had the questions to ask. You've probably been like many leaders who assume you have more authority when you tell others the answers instead of inviting them to be part of the solution.

There are many ways to use this little book. You can certainly read it cover-to-cover (it won't take you very long!). When you're getting ready for a meeting or a conversation with a specific person, go to the Categories and find the area you're looking for. If you're feeling a little down, go to the section called "About ME!". Or just open it randomly and pick a question and hold on to it. Maybe that's exactly what you need at just that moment.

Some of the questions appear in more than one category, and nearly all of them can certainly fit in the About ME section.

Skim through the questions and get familiar with how you would answer them for yourself before you try to use them as a "technique" with or on others.

Your authenticity in building your own awareness will take you far in learning to truly connect with people in all areas of your life.

AWARENESS +

ARTFUL ACTION/TIME =

TRANSFORMATION

About Learning

- What is possible?
- What do you mean?
- What is the part that is not clear yet?
- What needs to change in your thinking to take that action?
- If you were the bravest version of yourself today, what would you be doing?
- What are you tolerating right now in your life? What are you holding on to that you need to let go of?
- What would happen if you did nothing?
- What are you grateful for?
- Who is grateful for you?
- What do you think is best?

When no answer satisfies, and people continue to act as if they do not understand, then the wrong question is being asked.

-Peter Block

About Learning

- What is the cost of holding on to this problem? What is the payoff?

- Are you acting out of love or fear?

- How do you feel about the situation?

- What do you think it means?

- What other approaches can you think of?

- If you could do it over again, what would you do differently?

- Despite a particular failure, what would you do again anyway?

- Despite a particular success, what would you change?

- What is the lesson/message/problem/crisis?

- What is it that makes you come alive?

About Strategy

- What is your desired outcome?
- What is exciting to you about this?
- What do you think is best?
- What do you want? Are you interested or committed?
- What's missing, the presence of which would make a positive difference?
- How, specifically, will you know you've completed that action/goal?
- What's the first or easiest step you could take?
- Imagine your issue is solved. How did you get there?
- What's the problem in a nutshell? Now what's the problem in one sentence? What's the problem in one word?

What will matter most to us, upon deeper reflection, is the quality of experience we create in the world, not the quantity of results.

-Peter Block

About Strategy

- If you did know how to solve it, what would you try?

- What would you advise me to do if I had the problem you have?

- Which of your core values does this goal express?

- What do you need to say no to?

- Are you willing to do whatever it takes to obtain your objective?

- Are you willing to give up something to get there?

- What will be one result of you communicating your vision clearly to someone else?

About Addressing Difficult Situations

○ What are you avoiding?

○ What do you think is best?

○ How does it occur to you?

○ How does that serve you?

○ What's the easiest way forward?

○ How important is this to you, really?

○ When is the last time you were out of your comfort zone?

○ Is this a story or the truth? How can you find out?

About Addressing Difficult Situations

○ What does your gut tell you about this?

○ What rules do you have that are getting in the way?

○ What are you pretending not to know?

○ What would someone who has a very different set of beliefs than you do say about (your situation)?

○ What if you don't solve this problem in 6 months? What are the consequences?

○ In which situations is everything working fine and you don't have concerns or problems?

○ What is different about those situations?

There is always time to do everything that really matters. If we do not have time to do something, it is a sign that it does not matter.

-Peter Block

About Redirecting Others' Behavior

- What do you think is best?
- What resonates with you?
- What do you want? Are you interested or committed?
- Can you tell me more? What else?
- What is an example?
- What would you suggest I ask you to move this forward?
- How is what you are currently doing working to get what you say you want?
- What do you NOT want me to ask you?
- If you were the bravest version of yourself today, what would you be

About Redirecting Others' Behavior

- Is this a story or the truth? How can you find out?

- What does your gut tell you about this?

- Are you standing in your power or attempting to please someone else?

- Are you procrastinating or is there a reason to delay?

- What part of this is your responsibility?

- What's stopping you from taking new action?

- How is this serving you?

- How it is serving the world/World?

Be aware of the times you want to impress people with your brilliant knowledge. That's a perfect time for a powerful question.

About ME!

- What is my desired outcome?

- What am I pretending not to know?

- What's wrong with how I am right now and where am I already awesome?

- What haven't I admitted out loud yet?

- Is this really all I think I deserve?

- What am I tolerating right now in my life? Am I holding on to something I need to let go of?

- In what ways am I contributing to the problem – perhaps unintentionally?

- Is there some payoff I'm getting by holding on to my negative feeling? Is there possibility in letting it go?

- What could I be happy about if I chose

About ME!

- What keeps happening to me? Does it happen TO me or FOR me?

- Am I focused on what's wrong or what's right?

- Is that a story or the truth? How can I find out?

- Am I standing in my power or attempting to please someone else?

- Through whose eyes am I seeing this?

- Is this a blind spot for me?

- What causes me to get nervous or feel a lack of confidence?

- What questions am I asking myself when I am not feeling confident?

- How do I currently impact those around

Non-Questions

Some of the questions aren't questions at all, but they are conversation starters.

When you want to open a dialogue rather than close a deal or win an argument, use phrases like these:

- I have an idea …
- I'm wondering …
- It occurs to me …
- I could be completely wrong about this, but …
- Help me understand …
- Give me some feedback about the choices

The problem a person is telling you about isn't the real problem.

The real problem is their mindset, or how they are THINKING about the problem.

Albert Einstein told us that our current problems can't be solved from the same level of thinking that created them. To expect that we can do the same thing over and over and get different results is insanity.

When any of us truly believes our role is to fix someone else's problem, we're actually reinforcing that level of thinking that clearly isn't working.

Often we think we're being kind and helpful when we solve others' problems for them (or give them our advice even when they're not asking for it). But when we do this, we send them an unconscious message that we don't really believe they are capable of solving their own problems. Or maybe our egos feel better when we are doing something.

Instead of helping the situation, we actually take away the other person's ability to learn something. We make the other person dependent upon us, and then get resentful because he's doing exactly what we've set him up to do.

**There is another way.
Ask instead of tell.**

In your next 5
conversations,
pretend you know
nothing.

In Gratitude

This project would not have been born had it not been for my fantastic coaching clients who help me hone my questioning skills every day. So thank you to everyone who has trusted me over the years to help guide you on your journey. Little do you know we're actually making our way through together, and I learn just as much as you do!

Thanks also to Kelly Meyer, who dropped everything to help me work through these questions on a moment's notice. Love ya – mean it!

I'm eternally grateful for my MasterMind family. Thanks for doing life with me.

Appendix

On the morning of March 26, 2018 I posted this question on my Facebook page:

"I'm working on a project. What is the best/most impactful question anyone (including yourself) ever asked you?"

I had no idea that question would inspire such amazing results. In fact, they are still coming in as I finish this little book. So on the following pages are the unedited responses (except for spelling!) with permission from those who responded to use them in this book. I know you will find a plethora of wisdom in paging through them.

Lisa Renton Hudson What are you waiting for?

Kristine Freije Olson How has cancer changed you?

Marilyn McMurray If your child was you what advice would you give them at this moment....why aren't you taking your own advice?

Lee Roggenkamp What's your biggest challenge these days?

Amanda 'Mandee' McKinnon Are you a better person for having that person in your life?

Sue Racioppi Dericks Why do you care so much about me?

Jakelle Cornell Hoffmann What keeps you up at night?

Kara Meslow What's the common denominator?

Steph Bynum What would you do if you weren't afraid?

Kagey Gray What's your plan for retirement?

Connie Ihry Caspers Your husband has dementia Connie. What is your greatest challenge, what is your greatest blessing?

Jodie Harvala What is something that scares the shit out of you but you know you're going to do it anyway?

Laetitia Mizero Hellerud 1. What do you want your legacy to be? 2. What do you want to be remembered for when you are gone? 3. What values can't you compromise with? 4. Are you happy? Why?

Kristy Berger Jelinek If you could do anything for an entire day with no restrictions, what would it be? The reason it was so impactful was because the only answer I could come up with at that time was to sleep... This question was the start of my journey to self discovery all over again.

Aaron Hughes If you could start over, what would you do differently? What is your biggest regret?

Jacqueline McMillan What would you try to do if you weren't afraid of failure?

Jaime Berthelsen-Bartell If your family ceased to exist tomorrow if you didn't do what you needed to do, would you do it?

Carrie Knutson Does it make you happy?

Kay Wolf Powell What would it take for you to KNOW it was better? (or it got solved)

Jennifer Deich Grieve Is what you are doing making your life or someone else's life better?

Sara Kearns Stolt If you could have one do-over in your career what would it be? Why?

Babs Coler If you could do anything or be anything, what would that be?

Rebecca Jensen If you KNEW money was not an issue and everything you dreamed up came to you, what would your life look like?

Peter Weller What else?

Rebecca Rodine Undem How's that working for you? (When being challenged about something I'm holding on to that probably should be released...) It's very Dr. Phil but it does prove a point! I'm totally loving this thread BTW...

Natalie Sparrow What would make you happy?

DeLynne Lucus Bock Are you sure where you will spend eternity?

Dru Lee What evidence are you creating that you are heading in the direction you desire?

Beth Kosen-Judnick How are you making a difference in the world? Has your life been filled with joy? If you chose a different career path, what would it have been? What is your purpose? (Why are you here?)

Rohin Sachdeva What's the one thing I could do today to move forward? Then ask it everyday.

Doyle Lentz Are you making a difference ??

Liz Fevig Hager Who was your hero growing up?

Del Rae Williams If you knew you would succeed, what would you choose to do?

Linda J Hurst Between now and dead, what do you want your life to look like?

Tara Argall If you could have an easy way to find out the answers to your questions would you really want to know?

Hollie Lyons Savell Will that choice make a difference... positive/negative?

Carol Udart My favorite is "What's the object of the exercise?"

Heather Schmidt years ago, I was talking to a friend about the romantic relationship I was in at the time. It wasn't a question that changed me. "You have the right to be with someone who treats you poorly if that's what you want."

Julie Holgate What's the biggest risk you ever took?

Lauri Winterfeldt How's that working for you?...(said with love, not cynicism)

Michelle Heath Berg What is your why, or simply put, what do you want? It was a terrifying question at the time. You might remember, having been the one to ask! ☺

Lisa Hatlestad Why are you choosing to believe that you'll always struggle?

Susan Vitalis Who am I and what am I here for?

Deb Soland How are you? (And really caring if you are ok). Not just asking to make conversation.

Joey Minshall one that has helped me a lot ☺ "What would Love do right now?"

Kim Reichel Batterman If you could do one thing differently which you know would completely change your business what would it be? Then do it!

Laetitia Mizero Hellerud My 22 years old son likes to ask to people he just met for the first time. Instead of the habitual "hello" or "how are you?" he asks you an open-ended question. My favorites: 1. What inspires you? 2. What is your most recent epiphany? Last month he came with me to a conference in Bismarck and met one of my acquaintances. He must be approaching 80, a successful businessman who was an elected politician in his area back in the day. My son asked him: "What are your dreams?" He looked at him and teared up as he answered that question....It was beautiful!

Judy Johnson Felch Maybe not the most impactful…but my new son-in-law said he likes to ask people what their passion is...what they do love to do when they're not working. I like this...I've always enjoyed my work but some people don't and don't want to be defined by this especially if they've retired or stay at home parents or a victim of downsizing... I like this and now try to ask this.

Rita Visser What will make x seen as a success? On the other side of it, at what point do you have to find a different path to get the result you expected?

Lisa Prosen Is this what you want?

Jeff Voorhees Mine: Why?

Jenny Swain What are you up to?

Vincent Lindstrom My question, if I only have one is : What makes you happy?

Karissa LeAnn Brusseau How and When did you realize that it was your differences that were your gift?

Cyn Thia Do u have any children or what happened to them?

Kirsten Jensen What is the best compliment you've ever received?

Judi Bland Stull What is your Why? (That took me several years to actually figure out.)

Kelly Oevermann Elkin What haven't I asked you that I should? What do you have left to learn? What impact will this decision have on your life, a year from now?

Rachelle Turner If you knew you could not fail, what would you do with your life?

Lisa Battaglino-Nelson How can u shine ur light on the world?

Ashley Lunn What are you pretending not to know?

Andra Palmer What's your legacy?

Roxane Beauclair Salonen Will you marry me?

Lynn Dorn What is your greatest need?

Ann Braunagel Why is that important to you?

Ellen Curran Puffe What makes you happy?

Karen M Stensrud What do you need more of? (Turned out, it was time.)

Jodi Puhalla In 1973, I was in an ambulance after a plane crash and the young male paramedic asked me if he could cut my blue jeans to examine my leg. He waited for my consent. I was only 8 years old and I am not sure I have ever received that much respect for my body. I was just 8 years old and I had a broken femur bone but he waited patiently until I allowed this.

Dave Mortenson What is the airspeed of an unladen swallow?

Kari Warberg Block What will you do with your life?

Saree Reveling Where did that belief actually come from?

Dylan VonBank Mine is: "What is the best/most impactful question anyone (including yourself) ever asked you?" Because it forced me to actually think about it 😁

Kathy Parker Wegwert What's most important to you in your job or career?

Linda Novak Giannosa How do you want to impact the world?

Mary Jo Van Horn What is the lesson I am meant to learn?

Chelle Lyons Hanson What is the world's greatest need and what skill or talent do you have to contribute to addressing it?

Pete Seljevold What's your why?

<u>Holly O'Keefe</u> If time, money, and responsibilities were no object, what would you want to do over the next year?

<u>Beth Forkner Moe</u> What do you truly want to be doing with your life, five years from now? You're worth much more than you think you are or are being told.

<u>Tyler Schmidt</u> What am I capable of achieving?

<u>Sara Hockhalter</u> Was at a KW panel...someone asked the meaning of success...he replied...being anxiety free.

<u>Dale Lammi</u> After all you've experienced, have you ever had visions of your own death?

<u>Judy Dawson Einerson</u> What if it were easy?

<u>Tim Mathern</u> Will you be my mentor?

<u>Steve Schmitz</u> Is it in the best interest of the students?

<u>Melissa Simanek</u> If you me you in the street, what would be the first impression you'd leave yourself?

<u>Kelly Abrahamson Binfet</u> What have you learned from jobs that you never thought you would know?

<u>Tom Regan</u> What would you like inscribed on your tombstone?

<u>Chuck Hoge</u> What are you going to do for your Lord this year?

<u>Abby Tow</u> Who do you want to be?

The original question was "What was the best question someone asked <u>you</u>...." While not exactly following that format, these were great responses, too.

<u>Lee Hoedl</u> Question(s) I ask a group/individual to help them gain a greater perspective on their life are these and in this order: - If you only had 10 years to live, what would you be doing differently with your life from this time forward? - Now, if you had one year to live, what would you change in your life moving forward? - Now, if you only had one month live, what would you change with your life moving forward? Compare your answers between the first question and the third question. Now the major question: These changes that you mention, why aren't you doing them now?

<u>Jon Hegre</u> I was interviewing Babe Winkelman one time back in my TV days ...I asked him "If you were a fish what species would you be?" He laughed and said - "I have been on TV for over 30 years and interviewed by thousands and that is the best question anyone has ever asked me"- not sure if he was being truthful but he sure made me feel good.

Jodee
Bock

Jodee Bock is a dynamic business communicator, facilitator, speaker, trainer, and coach at her own company, Bock's Office Transformational Consulting. She helps organizations and individuals learn and grow in the areas of communication, leadership, and accountability.

Jodee is the author of several books including *The 100% Factor*, and the *Own Your Story* series. She is also the Regional Partner for the Dakotas and the Minnesota Regions of Master Networks.

She learns more every day and proves that coming from contribution and curiosity is a powerful way to add value to the lives of others.

Connect with Jodee through Facebook, Linked In or Twitter (@JodeeBock) or at her website www.bocksoffice.com.

Prayer From Napoleon Hill

I ask not, oh Divine Providence, for more riches but more wisdom with which to accept and use wisely the riches I received at birth in the form of the power to control and direct my mind to whatever ends I desire.

Feb.15.2021

Kolie,

Use this book to help you find your way in life. To help you direct shows. To help you create and find your intention As a way to connect with Other. Keep being mindfull and leaning into failure.

You've got a lot you will do
Find your lines and walk th

Be and be forward.
Kolle Shaw ♥

28725523R00033